Rainbow
ORIGAMI

CARLTON KiDS

ANNA BRETT

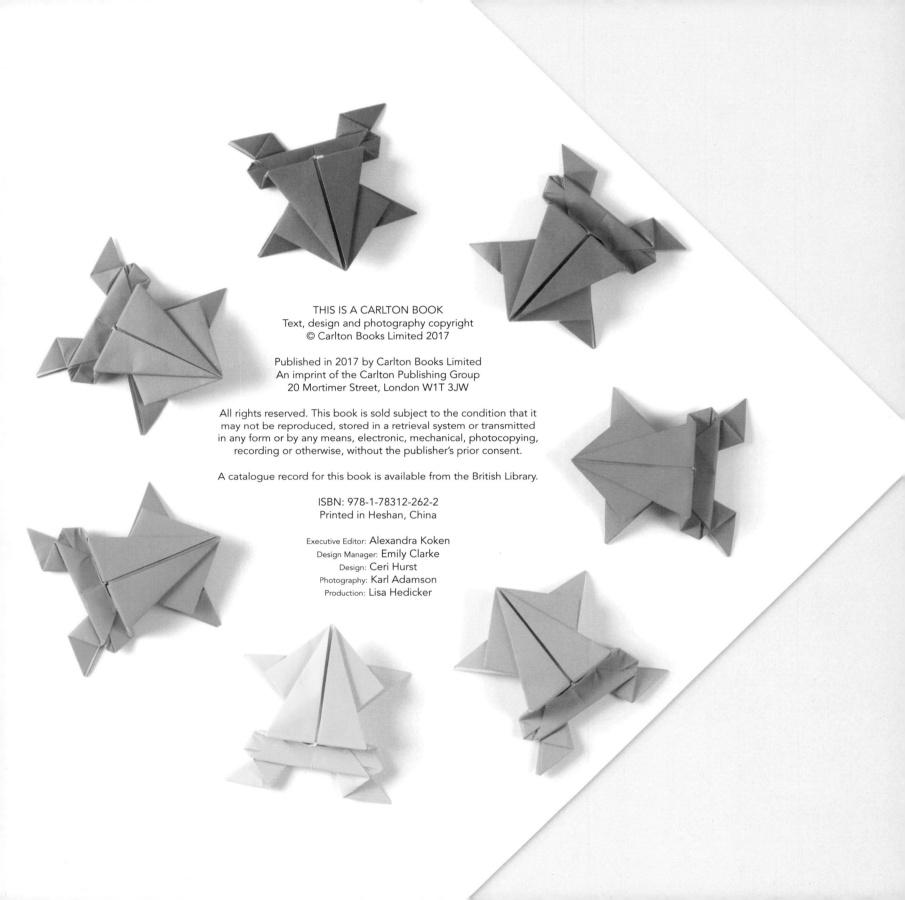

THIS IS A CARLTON BOOK
Text, design and photography copyright
© Carlton Books Limited 2017

Published in 2017 by Carlton Books Limited
An imprint of the Carlton Publishing Group
20 Mortimer Street, London W1T 3JW

A catalogue record for this book is available from the British Library.

ISBN: 978-1-78312-262-2
Printed in Heshan, China

Executive Editor: Alexandra Koken
Design Manager: Emily Clarke
Design: Ceri Hurst
Photography: Karl Adamson
Production: Lisa Hedicker

CONTENTS

Origami tips and tricks

Origami is the art of folding paper to make a model. It is an ancient Japanese practice that uses a single square piece of paper and just a handful of folding techniques. There's no cutting or sticking required! This book will show you how to make a heart, a butterfly, a boat, a fish, a bow, a frog, a flower and a crane. And by making your models in different colours you can create a fantastic rainbow effect!

You will discover how to make all eight models by following the simple steps, but before you begin it's worth familarizing yourself with the folds. Also learn about the the symbols that you will see alongside the photos, and some tips on how to make a good origami model.

Folds

There are three basic types of fold you need to know about, a valley fold, a mountain fold and a reverse fold. Practise them on a plain piece of paper if you wish.

1 **Valley fold**

For this you fold the paper up and over itself. This type of fold is named because it creates a valley in the paper.

It is represented by a dashed line.

2 **Mountain fold**

This type of fold makes a mountain of the paper as you fold it down and under itself.

It is represented by a dotted and dashed line.

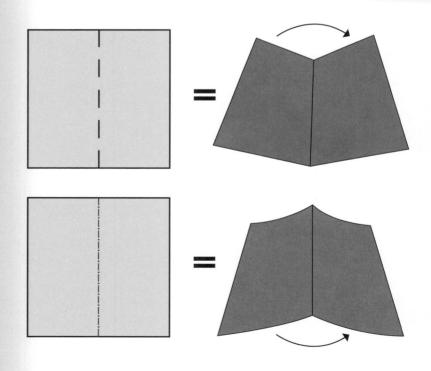

3 Reverse fold

You'll have to do a reverse fold to make the origami crane on page 43.

A. To begin the reverse fold first make a valley fold with your flap of paper.

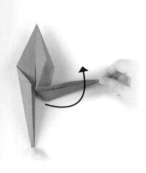

B. Then fold the flap you've just made in half with a mountain fold.

C. Push the tip down so it slots between the two edges of the flap.

D. Mountain fold the two outer edges of the flap at 45 degrees and press them together to make sure the fold forms a 'V' shape.

Symbols

Here are the symbols you will see alongside the photos to help explain what to do in each step.

 Fold in this direction

 Fold, crease, then unfold

 Turn the model over

 Repeat the folds you just made

 Push here, or squash or flatten the paper

 Rotate the model

Tips

★ The models have been graded beginner, confident and expert and although you can start with any model you like, it would be wise to start with the heart, which is a simple model, so you can get your confidence up.

★ Once you are ready to start a model, remember to carefully read the instructions and study the photo before beginning each step. Work on a flat surface as this will be much easier.

★ Fold as accurately as possible and always make sure you line up the edges and create crisp folds. Check what you are doing looks like the photo shown!

★ You can look ahead to the next step to see what is coming next, or go back a step if you've got lost or missed a fold by mistake. Above all, just keep going and within no time you'll be an origami master!

HEART

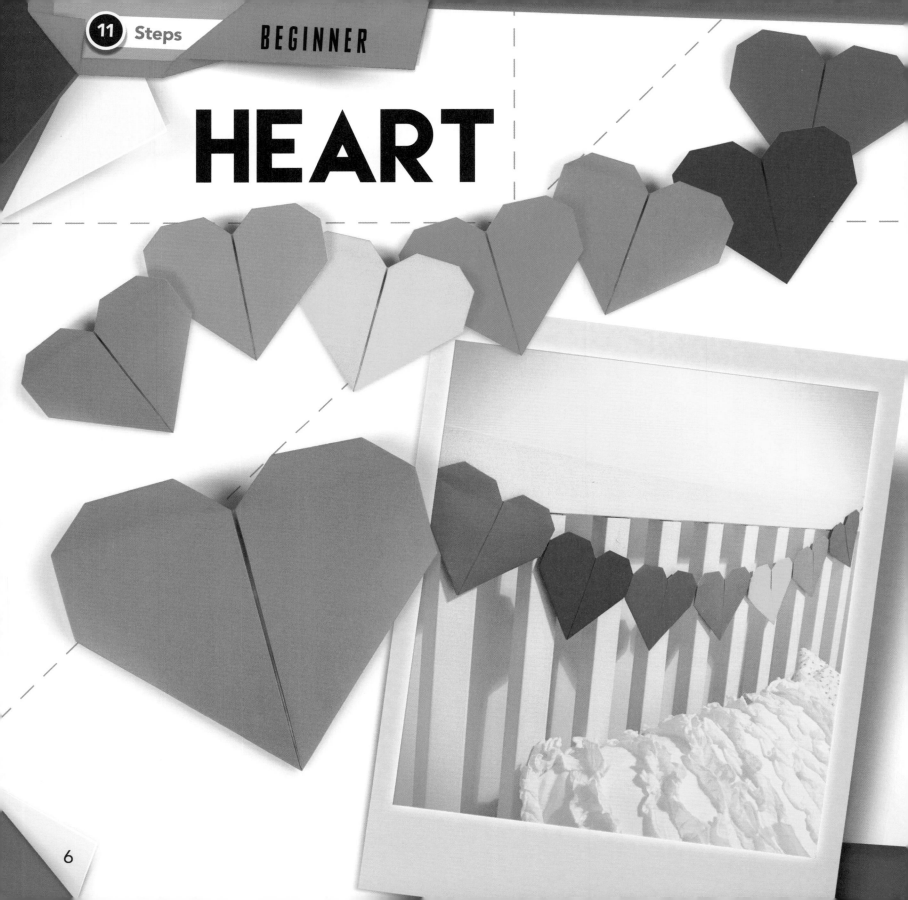

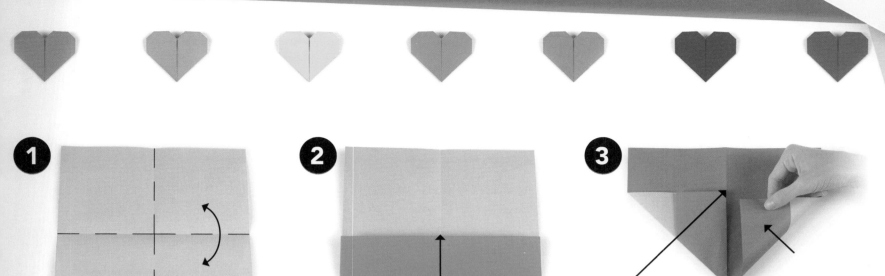

1 Place the paper colour-side down on your surface. Crease both centre lines of the square.

2 Fold the bottom edge up to align with the centre crease. Then turn the paper over.

3 Fold the bottom corners up to align with the centre crease. Then turn the paper over.

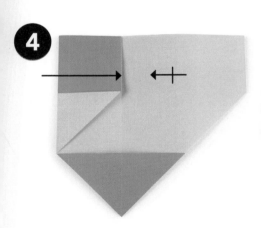

4 Take the top left edge and fold in towards the centre crease. Repeat with the top right edge.

Step 4 complete.

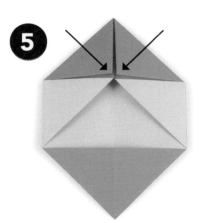

5 Fold the top corners down so the edges align with the centre crease.

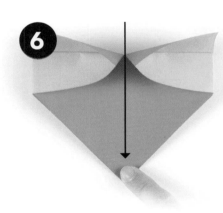

6 Fold the top tip down to meet the bottom tip of the model. You will now have two 3D flaps at the top of the model.

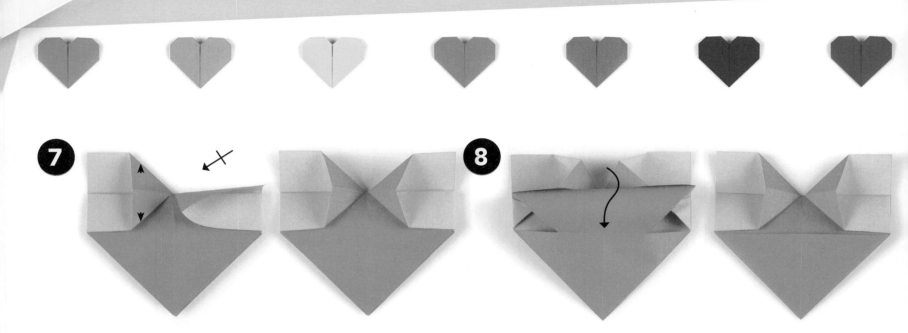

7 Push the outside edges of one 3D flap down so it lies flat, and align the central crease on the coloured side with the crease on the pale side. Repeat with the other flap.

Step 7 complete.

8 Holding the model at the bottom point, lift up the top layer to reveal a pocket on the bottom layer. Insert the top layer into the pocket then flatten the model.

Step 8 complete.

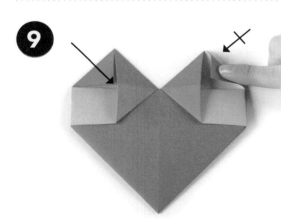

9 Take the top left corner and fold it down to meet the edge of the coloured triangle. Then repeat with the top right corner.

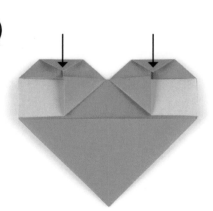

10 Fold down the top left tip of the model. Then repeat with the top right tip.

11 Turn the model over to reveal your finished heart.

HEART GARLAND

Once you have made several hearts in different rainbow colours, try making a pretty heart garland. Cut a piece of ribbon 60 cm long and lay it on a flat surface. Use tape to secure the ribbon to the backs of your hearts. Then tape the ends of your ribbon to a wall, or tie them wherever you like!

BUTTERFLY

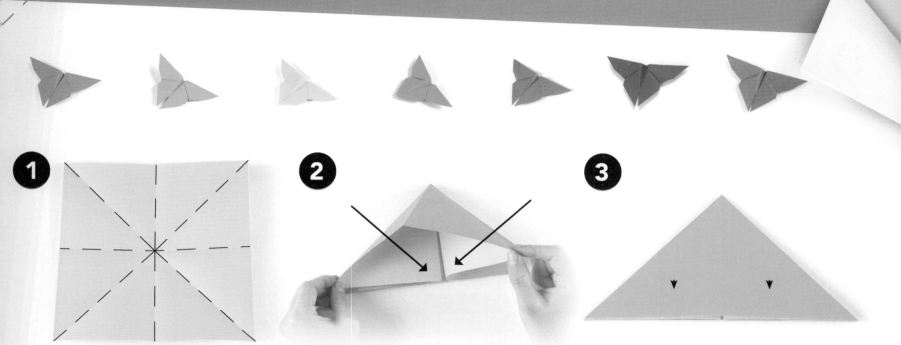

1 Place the paper colour-side down on your surface. Crease the two centre and two diagonal lines.

2 Take the left and right edges of the square and fold in and down towards the centre of the bottom edge.

3 Flatten the model.

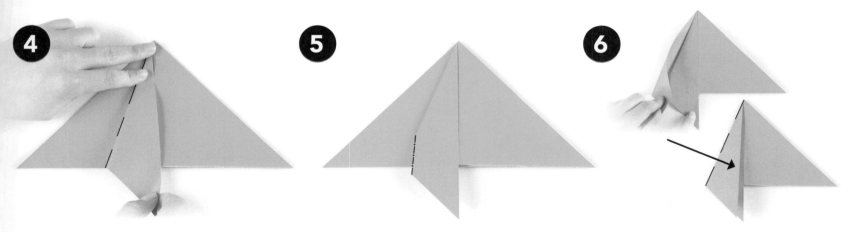

4 Take hold of the top layer of paper on the left side of the model and fold it over, bringing the outside edge to line up with the centre crease.

5 Fold back the outside tip of this new flap.

6 Take hold of the bottom layer of paper on the left side of the model and fold it over, bringing the outside edge to line up with the centre crease.

7

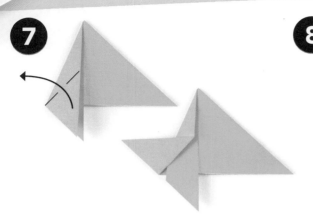

Fold the bottom tip of the top layer
of paper up and over itself.

8

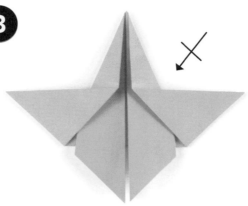

Now repeat steps 4-7
on the right side of the model.

9

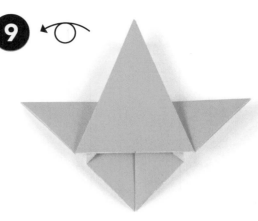

Turn the model over.

10

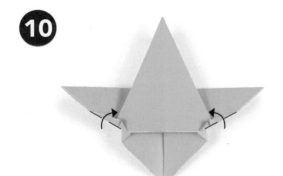

Fold the inside tips
of the wings inwards.

11

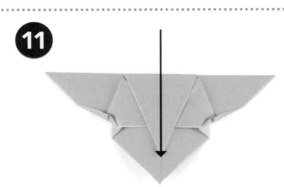

Take the top point of the model
and fold it down.

12

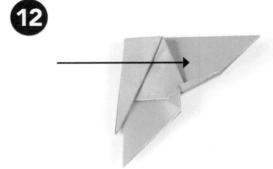

Fold the model in half.

13

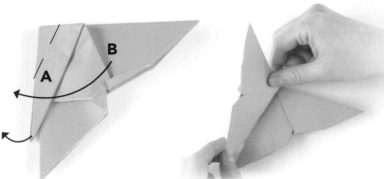

Ease out the body (labelled A) then
fold the top wing (labelled B) over and
crease along the dotted line as shown.

14

Repeat the fold on the second wing.
Open the wings up and your
butterfly is complete.

RAINBOW BUTTERFLY WALL

Make multiple butterflies with your rainbow origami paper and then stick their bodies to a wall to create a beautiful display.

CONFIDENT

BOAT

1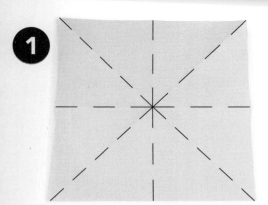

Place the paper colour-side down on your surface. Crease the two centre and two diagonal lines.

2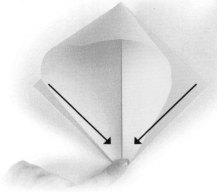

Rotate the paper so it is a diamond shape...

...then bring the two outer tips down and in to meet the bottom tip.

3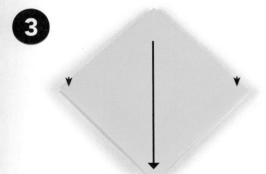

Bring the top tip of the diamond down to the bottom tip and flatten the sides so you have a smaller coloured diamond shape.

4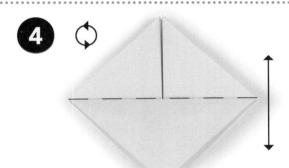

Rotate the paper 180 degrees so the open tip is at the top, then fold down the top point of the top sheet of paper to meet the bottom point. Unfold.

5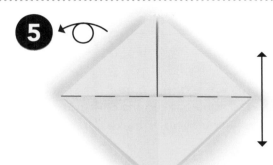

Turn the paper over and repeat step 4 by folding down the top point to meet the bottom point. Unfold.

6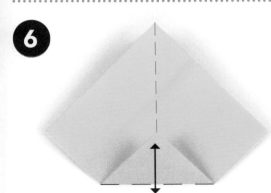

Fold the bottom point up to the centre crease, then unfold.

7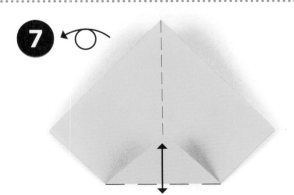

Flip the paper and fold the bottom point up to the centre crease again, then unfold.

8

Completely unfold the paper with the coloured side up.

15

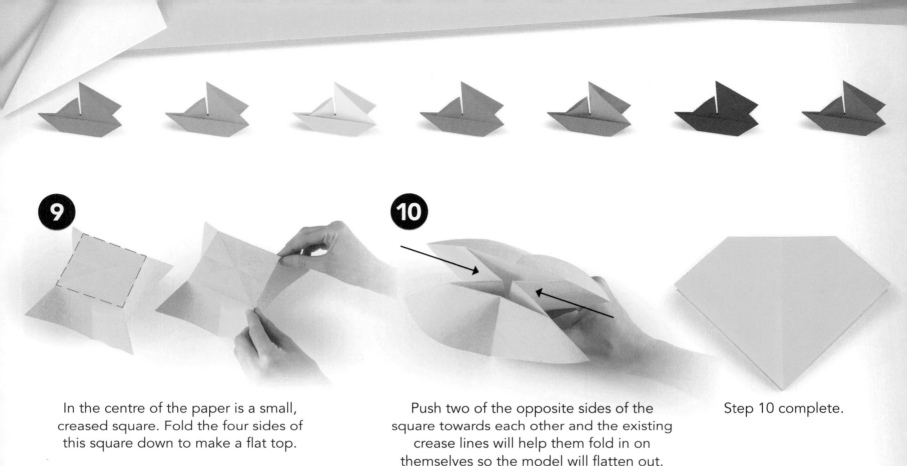

9

In the centre of the paper is a small, creased square. Fold the four sides of this square down to make a flat top.

10

Push two of the opposite sides of the square towards each other and the existing crease lines will help them fold in on themselves so the model will flatten out.

Step 10 complete.

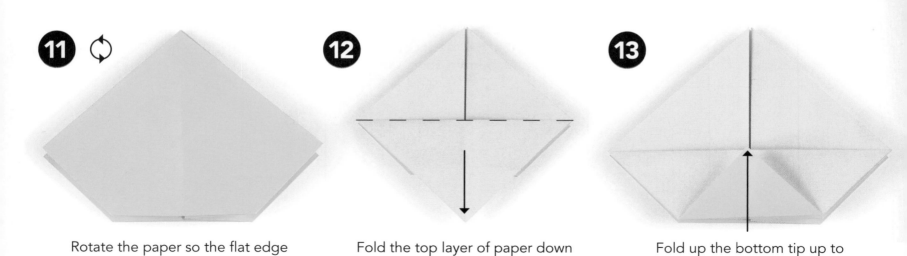

11 ↻

Rotate the paper so the flat edge sits at the bottom of the model.

12

Fold the top layer of paper down along the horizontal crease.

13

Fold up the bottom tip up to meet the horizontal crease.

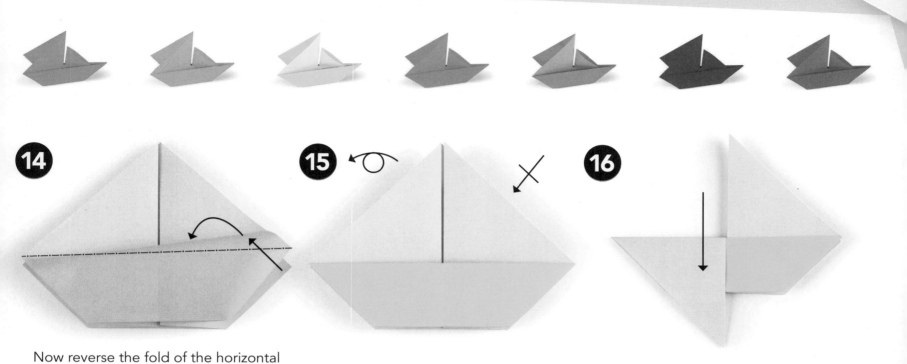

14 Now reverse the fold of the horizontal crease you made in step 12 so the flap tucks down inside the pocket at the base of the model.

15 Turn the model over and repeat steps 12, 13 and 14 on this side.

16 Fold the left sail down over the top of the coloured boat.

17 Fold the sail back on itself, around a finger's width lower than the fold you made in step 16.

18 Tuck the folded part of the sail inside the boat to hold it in position.

19 Widen the boat's base a little so it can stand up, ready to sail.

RAINBOW BOAT RACE

Make origami boats in rainbow colours, and take them out for a race on the water!

FISH

1

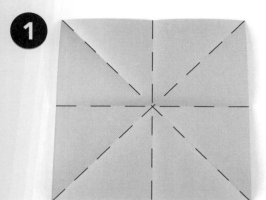

Place the paper colour-side down on your surface. Crease the two centre and two diagonal lines.

2

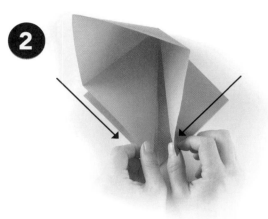

Rotate the paper so it is a diamond shape and take the two outer tips down and in to meet the bottom tip.

3

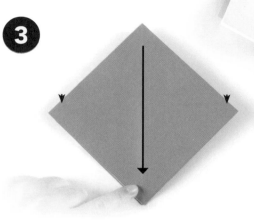

Bring the top tip of the diamond down to the bottom tip and fold in the sides so you have a smaller coloured diamond shape.

4

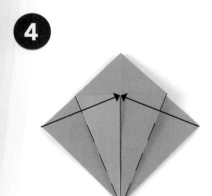

Fold the lower left edge of the diamond up to meet the centre crease then repeat with the lower right edge.

5

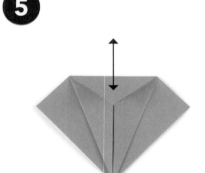

Fold the top point of the diamond down, crease and unfold. Unfold the flaps made in step 4 as well.

6

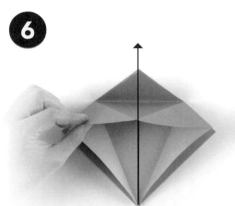

Bring the bottom point of the diamond up to open out the model and re-fold the creases made in steps 4 and 5 to flatten.

Fish 21

7

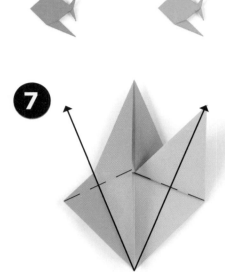

Fold up the top layers of paper on the left and right side of the model.

8

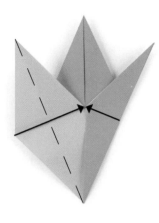

Fold both sides of the model in half so the edges meet along the centre.

9

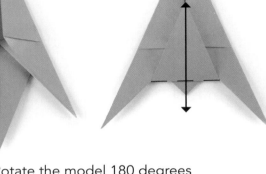

Rotate the model 180 degrees and fold up the bottom tip, crease then unfold.

10

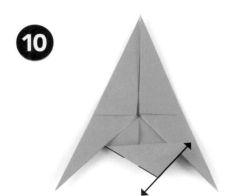

Fold the point up so the left edge is aligned with the crease you made in step 9. Unfold.

11

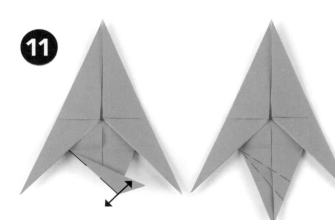

Fold the point up again so the left edge aligns with the crease you made in step 10. Unfold. You have now created two creases, shown above in red.

12

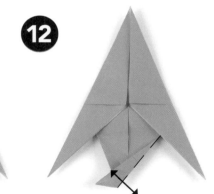

Fold the point up again, but this time mirror the fold made in step 11, creasing the paper in the opposite direction. Unfold.

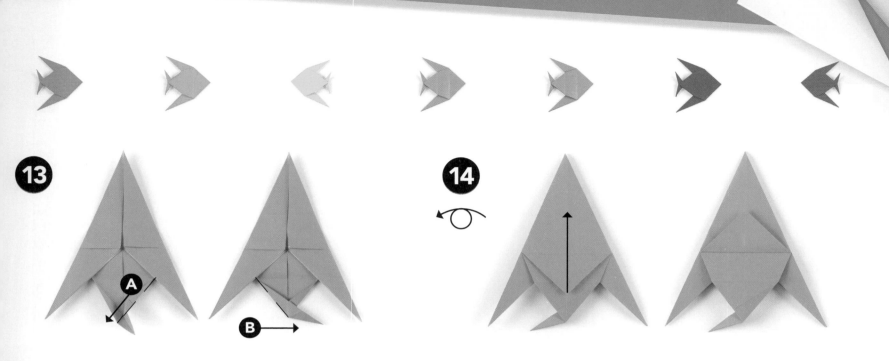

13 Begin to re-fold the crease made in step 12 (as shown on step 13A) but stop at the centre line and then fold the left side of the paper over the top, re-folding the crease you made in step 11 (as shown on step 13B).

14 Turn the model over and fold the triangular flap of paper up.

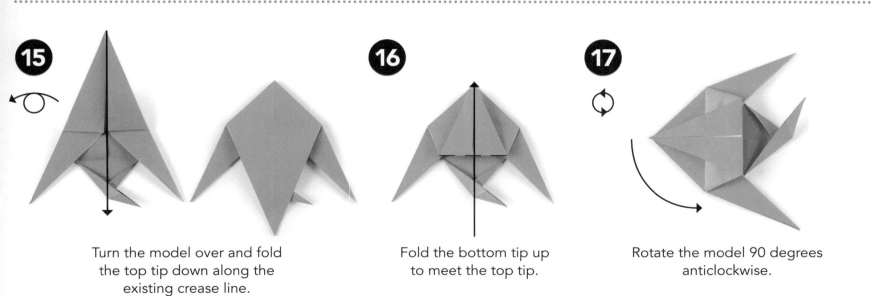

15 Turn the model over and fold the top tip down along the existing crease line.

16 Fold the bottom tip up to meet the top tip.

17 Rotate the model 90 degrees anticlockwise.

18

Fold the bottom
edge up to align with
the verticle edge.
Unfold.

19

Fold the bottom edge up
to align with the crease you
made in step 18. Unfold.
You have now created two
creases, shown above in red.

20

Fold the top edge down,
mirroring the fold you
made in step 19. Unfold.

21

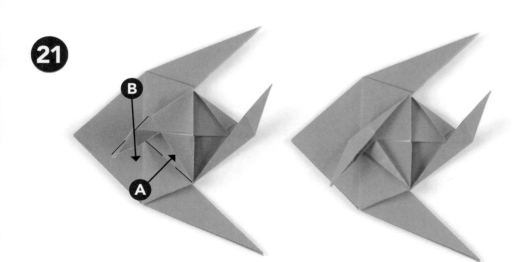

Begin to re-fold the crease made in step 19
(as shown in fold A) but stop at the centre point,
then re-fold the crease made in step 20
over the top (as shown in fold B).

22

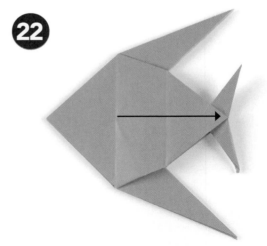

Fold over the flap you've been
working on and your fish is complete!

SHOAL OF TROPICAL FISH

Make origami fish in different rainbow colours. Stick each one to a wooden stick (try using a lolly stick or craft wire) and tape the sticks to a base such as the edge of a table or a windowsill. Vary the height of the fish so it looks like they are swimming in a shoal.

BOW

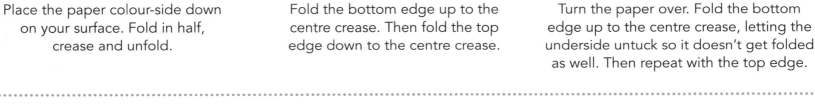

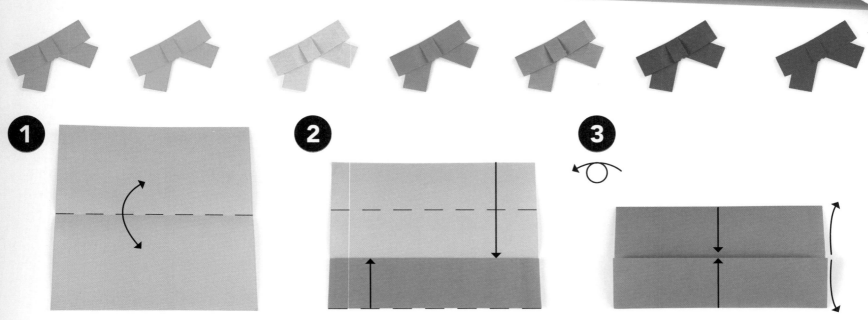

1 Place the paper colour-side down on your surface. Fold in half, crease and unfold.

2 Fold the bottom edge up to the centre crease. Then fold the top edge down to the centre crease.

3 Turn the paper over. Fold the bottom edge up to the centre crease, letting the underside untuck so it doesn't get folded as well. Then repeat with the top edge.

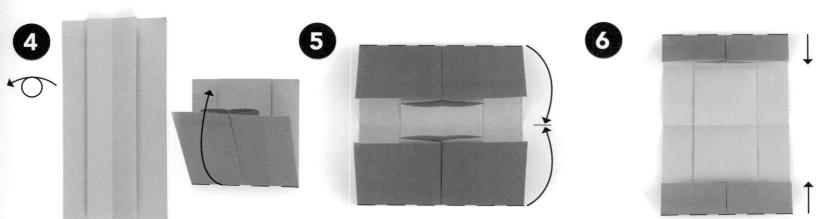

4 Turn the paper over. Fold in half vertically.

5 Unfold the paper, then fold the bottom edge up to the centre crease. Repeat by folding the top edge down to the centre crease.

6 Unfold the paper, then fold the bottom edge up to the quarter mark crease. Repeat by folding the top edge down to the three quarter mark crease.

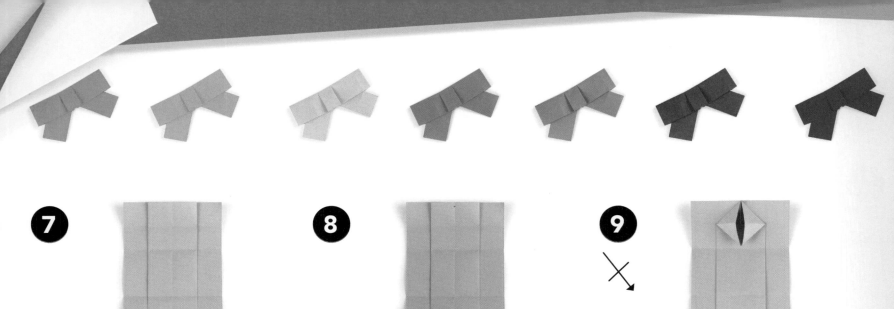

7  Unfold the paper, then 45-degree fold the two bottom corners of the flaps at the bottom of the model. Crease and unfold.

8  Open up the flap and then, by pushing the edges in towards each other, squash the flap flat to the model.

9 Repeat steps 7 and 8 at the other end of the model.

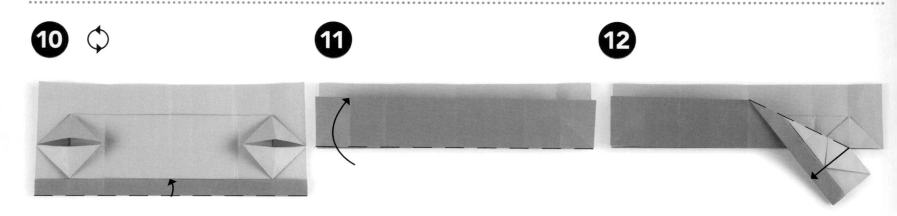

10 Turn the model 90 degrees and fold the bottom edge up to the bottom edge of the centre piece.

11 Fold the model along the centre crease.

12 Take the top half of the right edge of the model and fold down at a 45-degree angle.

28   Bow

13

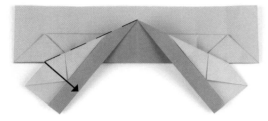

Repeat with the left edge, folding it down at a 45-degree angle.

14

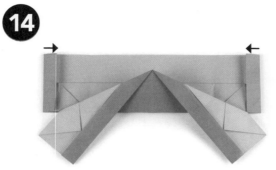

Fold the right edge in towards the first crease mark. Then repeat with the left edge, folding it in towards the first crease mark.

15

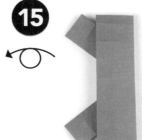

Turn the paper over and rotate it 90 degrees. Fold the bottom edge up, so that the edge of the bottom flap aligns with the edge of the top flap.

16

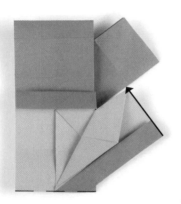

Unfold the paper and rotate the model 180 degrees. Repeat step 15, folding the bottom edge up so the edge of the bottom flap aligns with the edge of the top flap. Then unfold.

17

Turn the model over. Now, grab hold of the first crease line below the centre crease mark and pinch to lift up. Fold it over to line up with the centre crease.

18

Rotate the model 180 degrees and repeat step 17 by grabbing the first crease below the centre crease mark and pinch to lift up. Fold it over to line up with the centre crease.

19

Rotate the model 90 degrees and fold up the straight bottom edge to line up with the tip of your folded flaps.

20

Flip the model over and your bow is complete.

Make bows in different colours of the rainbow and use them as gift tags or decorations for presents.

FROG

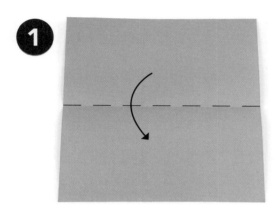

1 Place the paper colour-side down on your surface and fold in half.

2 Fold the paper in half again, crease then unfold.

3 On the right half of the paper, crease and unfold the two centre lines and the two diagonals.

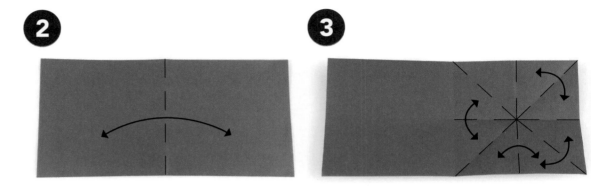

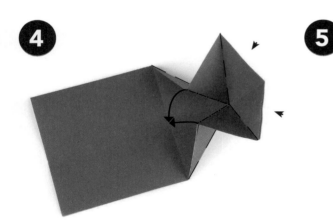

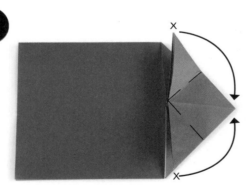

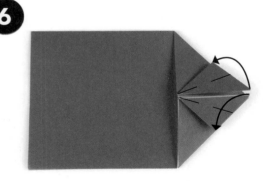

4 Take the middle of the top and bottom edges of the creased side of the paper and fold in to meet in the centre of the left side. Flatten the model.

5 Fold the edges of the top flap of paper up towards the point so the 'X's marked in the picture meet up.

6 Fold the tips of the flaps you made in step 5 back over on themselves so the edges line up.

7

Repeat steps 3 to 6
on the other side.

8

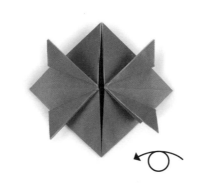

Your model should look like this.
Now turn it over.

9

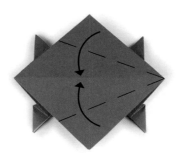

Fold the two outer edges in
to line up along the horizontal
centre of the model.

10

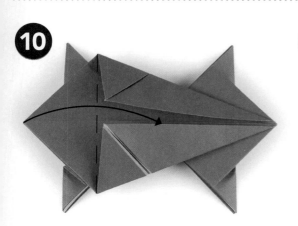

Fold the back tip up and over
the flaps you made in step 9.

11

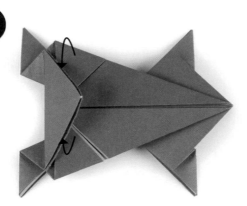

Tuck the edges of the flaps
you made in step 9 into the slits in
the pocket you folded in step 10.

12

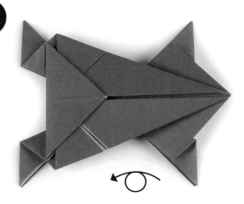

Your model should look like this.
Turn it over.

13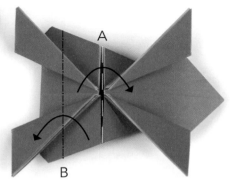

Fold the model in half along the centre line (A), then fold the back half of the model in half to create a zig zag fold (B).

14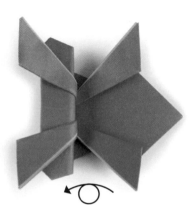

Your model should look like this. Turn it over.

15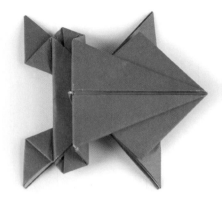

Your origami frog is complete!

Make your frog hop!

1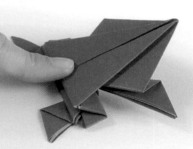

Press down gently on the back of the frog...

2

...to make him hop...

3

...into the air!

FROG HOP GAME

Make seven frogs in different rainbow colours to play this game. You can play on your own, or with six friends, and all you'll need is some chalk! Head outside and draw coloured rings on the ground, one inside the other, with a bullseye at the centre.

Now place the frogs around the outside of the biggest chalk ring and take it in turns to hop your frogs into the rings.

The frog that hits the bullseye wins!

FLOWER

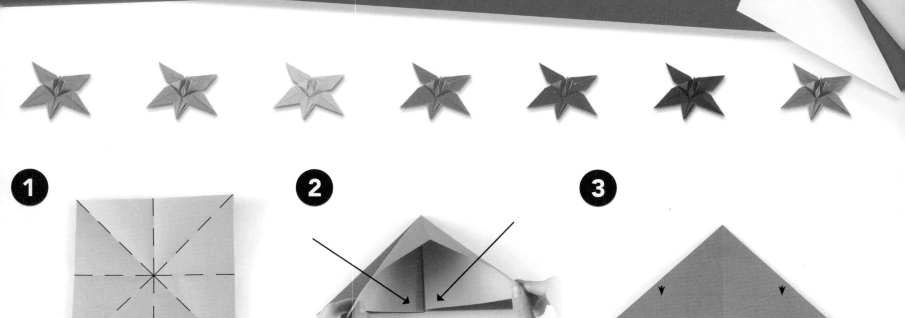

1

Place the paper colour-side down on your surface. Crease the two centre and two diagonal lines.

2

Take the left and right edges of the square and fold in and down towards the centre of the bottom edge.

3

Flatten the model.

4

Take the right edge of the top layer of the triangle and bring it up and then push the crease line down to align with the centre crease on the triangle.

5

Squash to flatten the model.

6

Turn the right half of the diamond you have just created over on itself to fold in half, creasing it along the centre line.

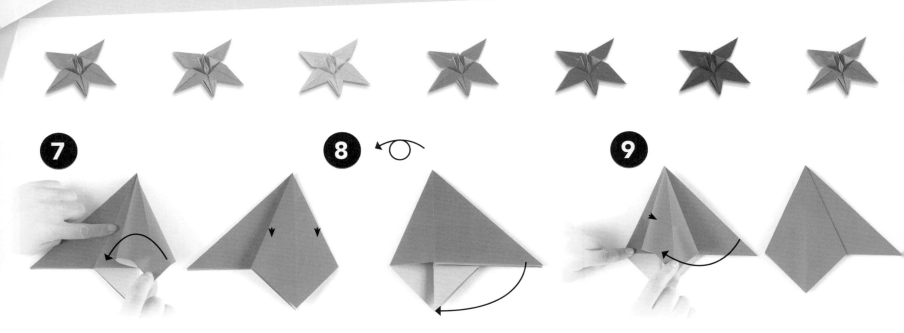

7

Take the right edge of the triangle and bring it up and then push the crease line down to align with the centre crease on the triangle, as you did in step 4. Squash to flatten.

8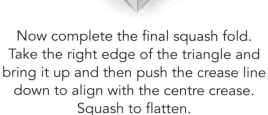

Turn the model over and repeat the squash fold again by taking the right edge of the top layer of the triangle and bringing it up...

9

...then pushing the crease line down to align with the centre crease on the triangle.

10

Turn the right half of the new diamond shape over on itself to fold in half, folding it along the centre line, as you did in step 6.

11

Now complete the final squash fold. Take the right edge of the triangle and bring it up and then push the crease line down to align with the centre crease. Squash to flatten.

12

Take the top piece of paper from the left side of the diamond shape and fold up and over to line the edge up with the centre crease.

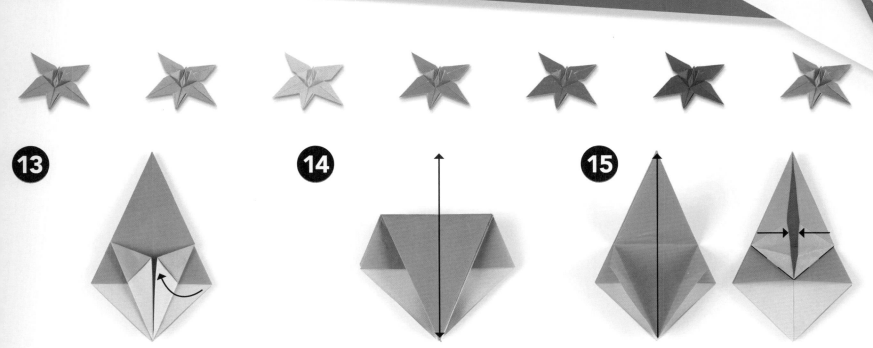

13

Repeat this fold on the right side.

14

Fold down the top point to meet the bottom point. Unfold this and the folds made in steps 12 and 13.

15

Lift the top layer of paper at the bottom and bring the tip up to meet the top tip, re-folding the creases you made in steps 12, 13 and 14. Flatten the model.

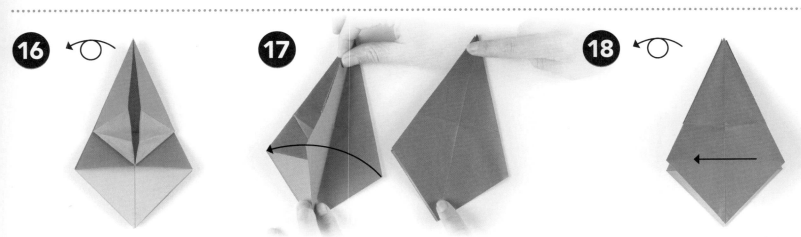

16

Turn the model over and repeat steps 12 to 15 on this side.

17

Take the top layer of paper on the right and fold over to show the third side of the original diamond.

18

Turn the model over, and then repeat step 17 by taking the top layer of paper on the right and folding over to show the fourth side of the original diamond.

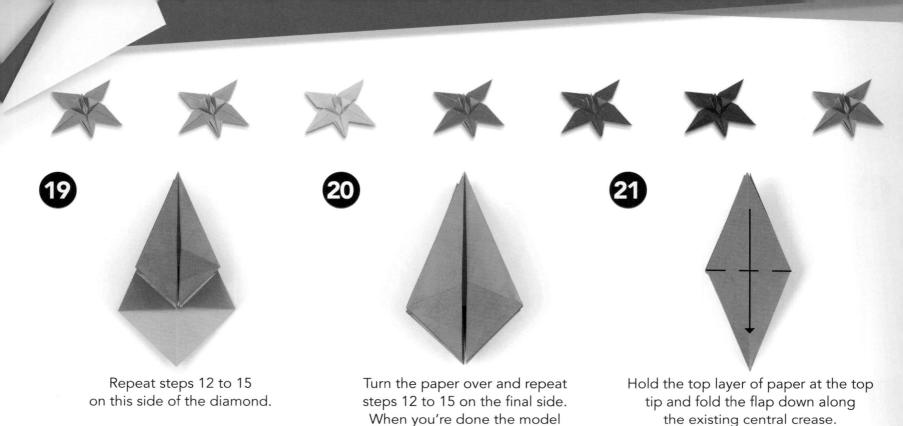

19 Repeat steps 12 to 15
on this side of the diamond.

20 Turn the paper over and repeat
steps 12 to 15 on the final side.
When you're done the model
should look like this.

21 Hold the top layer of paper at the top
tip and fold the flap down along
the existing central crease.

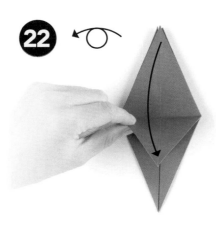

22 Turn the paper over and repeat
by folding the top tip of the
outer layer down along the
existing central crease.

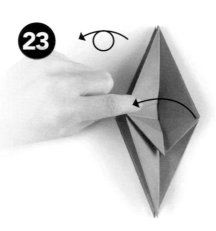

23 Take hold of the first and second
layers of paper on the right edge
of the diamond and turn over.
Then turn the model over and
repeat turning the first two layers on
the right edge of the diamond over.

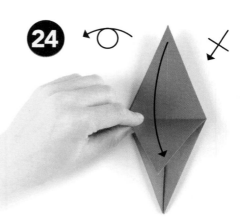

24 Fold the top tip of the outer layer down.
Then turn the model over and
repeat folding the top tip
down for the fourth time.

25 With the open end of the diamond at the bottom, fold the left and right corners of the diamond in and down to meet the centre crease.

26 Turn the model over and repeat step 25.

27 Fold over the sides of the model as you've done before to reveal sides three and four and repeat step 25 on these.

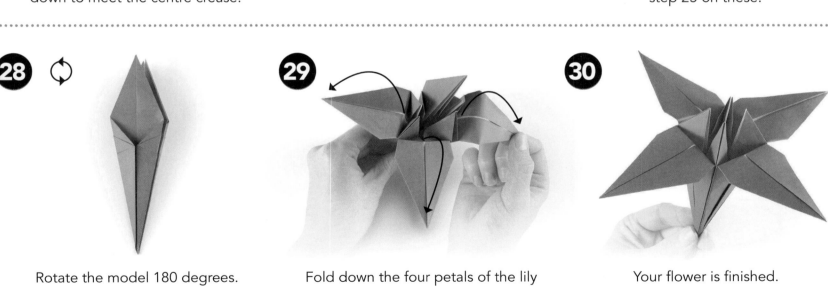

28 Rotate the model 180 degrees.

29 Fold down the four petals of the lily one by one and curve the tips slightly to shape them.

30 Your flower is finished.

Make beautiful flowers from different-coloured origami paper and then bunch them together in a bouquet!

Use craft wire or twigs and poke it in the bottom of each flower. Then arrange your rainbow of flowers in a vase!

CRANE

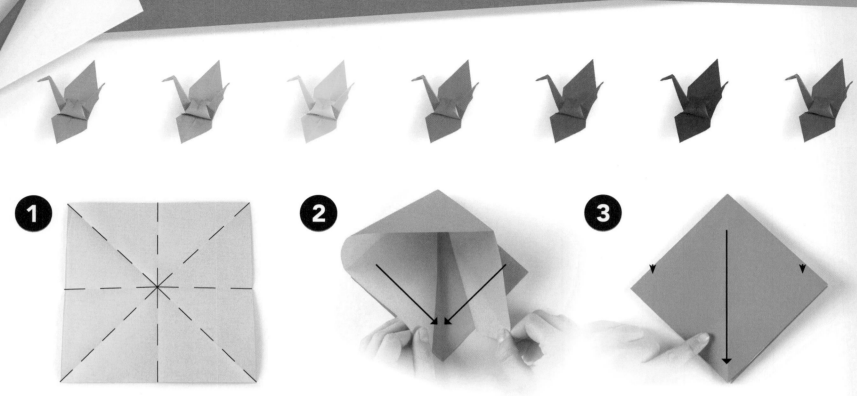

1
Place the paper colour-side down on your surface. Crease the two centre and two diagonal lines.

2
Rotate the paper so it is a diamond shape and take the two outer tips down and in to meet the bottom tip.

3
Bring the top tip of the diamond down to the bottom tip and fold in the sides so you have a smaller coloured diamond shape.

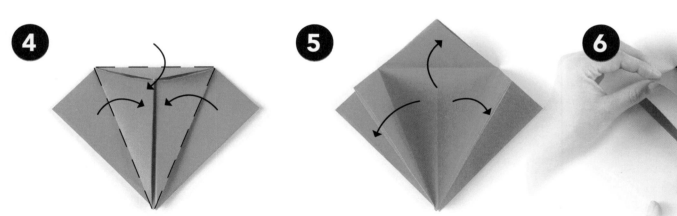

4
Take the top layer of paper and fold the edges in to line up with the centre crease. Then fold the top down.

5
Unfold the flaps you made in step 4.

6
Lift the front layer of paper up and refold the creases you made in step 4.

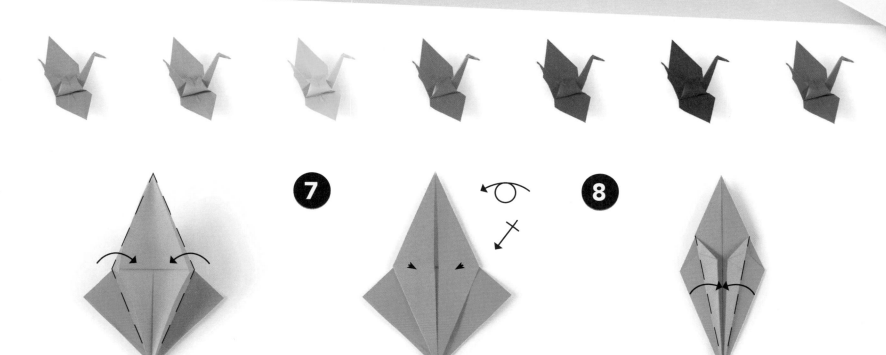

This shows step 6 in progress.

7 Press flat to create a long diamond shape. Then repeat steps 4 to 7 on the reverse of the model.

8 Take the top layer of paper and fold the edges in to line up with the centre crease.

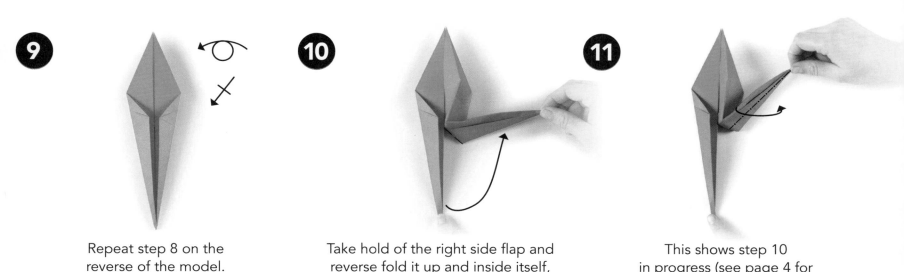

9 Repeat step 8 on the reverse of the model.

10 Take hold of the right side flap and reverse fold it up and inside itself, creasing along the dotted line shown.

11 This shows step 10 in progress (see page 4 for tips on how to reverse fold).

Crane   45

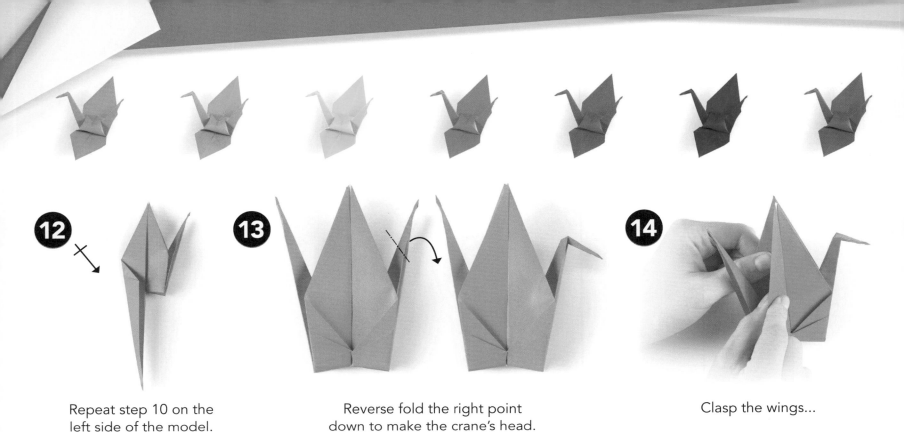

12 Repeat step 10 on the left side of the model.

13 Reverse fold the right point down to make the crane's head.

14 Clasp the wings...

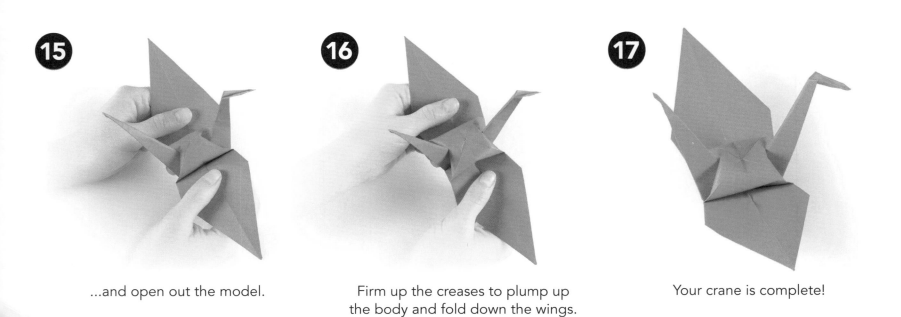

15 ...and open out the model.

16 Firm up the creases to plump up the body and fold down the wings.

17 Your crane is complete!

RAINBOW CRANE MOBILE

Once you've made origami cranes in different colours of the rainbow you can use them to create a mobile. You will need a circular mobile frame (which you can buy from a craft shop or make yourself by bending a wire hanger or tying twigs together into a hoop) and a needle and thread.

Ask an adult to push the thread through the crane's body and secure the end by tying a large knot. Tie the other end of the thread around the top of the frame. Repeat the process with the other cranes, varying the length of the thread to change the height of the cranes. Tie some ribbon to the frame and hang it up high.